Hearing Aids

The Ultimate Guide

Jills K Kurian

Copyright © 2023

Dedication

This book is dedicated to all those who have experienced the challenges of hearing loss, and the impact it can have on their quality of life. To those who have persevered, sought help, and found ways to manage their hearing loss, we honor your courage, resilience, and determination.

To the families, friends, and loved ones who have supported and encouraged those with hearing loss, we acknowledge and thank you for your unwavering love and patience.

To the audiologists, hearing aid specialists, and other healthcare professionals who have dedicated their lives to helping others with hearing loss, we express our gratitude for your compassion, expertise, and unwavering commitment to your patients.

May this book serve as a valuable resource for all those who struggle with hearing loss, providing information, support, and encouragement to help you live your best life. Together, we can break down the stigma surrounding hearing loss and create a more inclusive and accessible world for all.

Table of Contents

Chapter 1: Understanding Hearing Loss

Introduction:

Hearing loss is a common condition that affects millions of people worldwide. It can be caused by a variety of factors, including aging, exposure to loud noises, genetics, and certain medical conditions. Understanding hearing loss is the first step in finding the right solutions to improve your quality of life.

Types of Hearing Loss:

There are three main types of hearing loss: conductive, sensorineural, and mixed hearing loss. Conductive hearing loss occurs when sound waves are blocked from reaching the inner ear. This can be caused by a variety of factors, including ear infections, earwax buildup, and tumors. Sensorineural hearing loss occurs when there is damage to the inner ear or auditory nerve. This can be caused by aging, exposure to loud noises, and certain medical conditions. Mixed hearing loss is a combination of conductive and sensorineural hearing loss.

Causes of Hearing Loss:

The most common cause of hearing loss is age-related hearing loss, also known as presbycusis. This occurs naturally as we age and can begin as early as our 30s or 40s. Other causes of hearing loss include exposure to loud noises, genetics, ear infections, head injuries, and certain medical conditions, such as diabetes and heart disease.

The Impact of Hearing Loss on Your Life:

Hearing loss can have a significant impact on your quality of life. It can make it difficult to communicate with others, participate in social activities, and enjoy everyday experiences. It can also lead to feelings of isolation, anxiety, and depression. In some cases, hearing loss can also impact your ability to work and earn a living.

If left untreated, hearing loss can also lead to cognitive decline, as the brain begins to rewire itself in response to the lack of auditory input. This can result in a higher risk of developing dementia and other cognitive disorders.

Conclusion:

Understanding hearing loss is the first step in finding the right solutions to improve your quality of life. Whether you are experiencing mild or severe hearing loss, there are many solutions available to help you. By taking the time to learn about hearing loss and seeking the help you need, you can take control of your life and enjoy all of the sounds and experiences that the world has to offer.

Chapter 2: Benefits of Using Hearing Aids

Introduction:

Hearing aids are small electronic devices that are designed to amplify sound and improve the ability to hear. They are a common solution for people with hearing loss and offer many benefits to users. In this chapter, we will discuss how hearing aids work, the benefits of using hearing aids, how to choose the right hearing aid for your needs, and understanding the features of hearing aids.

How Hearing Aids Work:

Hearing aids work by capturing sound waves and amplifying them before they reach the inner ear. They consist of a microphone, an amplifier, and a speaker. The microphone captures sound waves and converts them into electrical signals, which are then amplified by the amplifier. The speaker then converts the amplified signals back into sound waves, which are delivered to the inner ear.

Benefits of Using Hearing Aids:

There are many benefits to using hearing aids, including:

Improved communication: Hearing aids can significantly improve communication with others, both in quiet and noisy environments.

Better quality of life: Hearing aids can improve the overall quality of life for people with hearing loss, allowing them to enjoy everyday experiences that they may have otherwise missed out on.

Increased safety: Hearing aids can improve safety by allowing people with hearing loss to hear warning signals, such as smoke alarms and car horns.

Enhanced social interaction: Hearing aids can help people with hearing loss to better participate in social activities, reducing feelings of isolation and loneliness.

Choosing the Right Hearing Aid for You:

Choosing the right hearing aid is important to ensure that you get the most benefit from using it. Factors to consider when choosing a hearing aid include:

Degree of hearing loss: The severity of your hearing loss will determine the type and style of hearing aid that is most appropriate for you.

Lifestyle: Consider your daily activities and the environments in which you will be using your hearing aid. This will help you choose a hearing aid with the appropriate features.

Budget: Hearing aids can be expensive, so consider your budget when choosing a hearing aid. There are many options available at different price points.

Understanding Hearing Aid Features:

Hearing aids come with many different features, including directional microphones, noise reduction, and feedback suppression. It's important to understand these features and how they can benefit you. For example, directional microphones can help you hear better in noisy environments, while noise reduction can help reduce background noise.

Conclusion:

Hearing aids offer many benefits to people with hearing loss, including improved communication, better quality of life, and increased safety. By choosing the right hearing aid and understanding its features, you can get the most out of using it. Remember, hearing loss is a common problem, and there is no shame in seeking help. With the right support and resources, you can overcome the challenges of hearing loss and enjoy all of the sounds and experiences that life has to offer.

Chapter 3: Getting Started with Hearing Aids

If you think you may have hearing loss, it's important to seek help from an audiologist. They can help determine the severity of your hearing loss and recommend the best solution for your needs. In this chapter, we will discuss how to make an appointment with an audiologist, getting a hearing test, understanding your hearing test results, and choosing the right hearing aid style and fit.

Making an Appointment with an Audiologist:

To get started with hearing aids, the first step is to make an appointment with an audiologist. You can find an audiologist through your primary care physician or by doing an online search. When you make your appointment, be sure to ask what you need to bring to your appointment, such as your medical history and any current medications you are taking.

Getting a Hearing Test:

During your appointment, your audiologist will perform a hearing test to determine the severity of your hearing loss. The test will consist of a series of sounds played at different volumes and frequencies. You will be asked to indicate when you hear the sounds. The results of your hearing test will be used to determine the type and severity of your hearing loss.

Understanding Your Hearing Test Results:

After your hearing test, your audiologist will discuss your test results with you. They will explain the type and severity of your hearing loss and make recommendations for the best hearing aid options for your needs. They may also discuss any additional medical conditions that may be contributing to your hearing loss.

Choosing the Right Hearing Aid Style and Fit:

Once you have decided to get hearing aids, your audiologist will work with you to choose the right hearing aid style and fit. There are several different types of hearing aids, including behind-the-ear, in-the-ear, and completely-in-the-canal. Your audiologist will help you choose the right style based on your lifestyle and hearing needs.

It's also important to choose the right fit for your hearing aid. Your audiologist will take measurements of your ear to ensure a comfortable and secure fit. They may also recommend additional features, such as directional microphones or noise reduction, to improve your hearing experience.

Getting started with hearing aids can be a daunting process, but with the help of an audiologist, it can be a smooth and successful experience. By making an appointment with an audiologist, getting a hearing test, understanding your hearing test results, and choosing the right hearing aid style and fit, you can take the first steps towards improving your quality of life with hearing aids. Remember, hearing loss is a common problem, and there is no shame in seeking help. With the right support and resources, you can overcome the challenges of hearing loss and enjoy all of the sounds and experiences that life has to offer.

Chapter 4: Adjusting to Your New Hearing Aids

Adjusting to new hearing aids can take time and patience. It's important to remember that it's a process, and it may take some time to get used to your new hearing aids. In this chapter, we will discuss understanding how hearing aids work, tips for adjusting to your new hearing aids, common challenges when using hearing aids, and troubleshooting hearing aid issues.

Understanding How Hearing Aids Work:

Before you begin using your hearing aids, it's important to understand how they work. Your audiologist can provide you with detailed instructions on how to use and care for your hearing aids. It's important to follow these instructions carefully to ensure that your hearing aids work effectively.

Tips for Adjusting to Your New Hearing Aids:

Adjusting to your new hearing aids can take time, but there are several tips that can help you get used to them more quickly. These include:

Wear your hearing aids consistently: Wear your hearing aids as often as possible to get used to them. This will also help your brain adjust to the new sounds.

Start in a quiet environment: Begin using your hearing aids in a quiet environment, such as at home. This will allow you to get used to the sounds without the distraction of background noise.

Increase volume gradually: Gradually increase the volume of your hearing aids over time. This will help your brain adjust to the new sounds more easily.

Practice listening skills: Practice listening skills, such as focusing on one person's voice in a noisy environment. This will help you get used to hearing in different environments.

Common Challenges When Using Hearing Aids:

There are several common challenges that people face when using hearing aids. These include:

Discomfort or pain: Your hearing aids may cause discomfort or pain, especially during the adjustment period. Be sure to communicate any discomfort or pain to your audiologist.

Feedback or whistling: Your hearing aids may produce feedback or whistling sounds. This can be caused by a poor fit or other issues.

Difficulty hearing in noisy environments: Hearing aids may not be effective in noisy environments, and you may still have difficulty hearing in these situations.

Troubleshooting Hearing Aid Issues:

If you experience any issues with your hearing aids, it's important to troubleshoot the problem. This may involve adjusting the fit or volume, cleaning the hearing aids, or replacing the batteries. If you are unable to resolve the issue on your own, contact your audiologist for assistance.

Adjusting to new hearing aids can be a process, but with patience and practice, you can get used to them quickly. By understanding how hearing aids work, following tips for adjusting to your new hearing aids, and troubleshooting any issues that arise, you can get the most benefit from using your hearing aids. Remember, hearing loss is a common problem, and there is no shame in seeking help. With the right support and resources, you can overcome the challenges of hearing loss and enjoy all of the sounds and experiences that life has to offer.

Chapter 5: Taking Care of Your Hearing Aids

Taking care of your hearing aids is essential to ensure that they work effectively and last for as long as possible. In this chapter, we will discuss cleaning and maintaining your hearing aids, replacing batteries and other parts, storing your hearing aids, and tips for extending the life of your hearing aids.

Cleaning and Maintaining Your Hearing Aids:

Cleaning your hearing aids regularly is important to prevent wax buildup and other debris from interfering with their performance. Use a soft, dry cloth to wipe down the exterior of your hearing aids every day. You can also use a specialized hearing aid cleaning kit to clean the small openings and other hard-to-reach areas. Avoid using water or other liquids to clean your hearing aids, as this can damage them.

Replacing Batteries and Other Parts:

Most hearing aids use batteries that need to be replaced periodically. Your audiologist can show you how to replace the batteries in your hearing aids. It's also important to replace other parts, such as tubing or ear molds, when necessary. Your audiologist can provide you with replacement parts and show you how to replace them.

Storing Your Hearing Aids:

When you're not wearing your hearing aids, it's important to store them properly to prevent damage. Store them in a cool, dry place, away from moisture and direct sunlight. You can also use a specialized hearing aid storage case to protect your hearing aids when they're not in use.

Tips for Extending the Life of Your Hearing Aids:

There are several things you can do to extend the life of your hearing aids, including:

Keep them dry: Avoid exposing your hearing aids to moisture or humidity, as this can damage them.

Remove them when using hair products: Hair products, such as hairspray, can damage your hearing aids. Be sure to remove them before using hair products.

Avoid exposing them to extreme temperatures: Don't leave your hearing aids in a car or other hot or cold environment, as this can damage them.

Schedule regular maintenance: Regular maintenance by your audiologist can help keep your hearing aids in good working condition.

Taking care of your hearing aids is essential to ensure that they work effectively and last for as long as possible. By cleaning and maintaining your hearing aids, replacing batteries and other parts when necessary, storing your hearing aids properly, and following tips for extending their life, you can get the most out of using your hearing aids. Remember, hearing loss is a common problem, and there is no shame in seeking help. With the right support and resources, you can overcome the challenges of hearing loss and enjoy all of the sounds and experiences that life has to offer.

Chapter 6: Maximizing Your Hearing Aid Experience

Hearing aids can significantly improve your ability to hear and communicate, but it's important to use them effectively to get the most benefit. In this chapter, we will discuss communicating effectively with hearing aids, participating in social activities with hearing aids, using assistive listening devices with hearing aids, and tips for making the most of your hearing aid experience.

Communicating Effectively with Hearing Aids:

Effective communication is essential for hearing aid users. When communicating with others, it's important to face them directly and maintain eye contact. Speak clearly and avoid speaking too quickly. If you're having difficulty understanding someone, don't be afraid to ask them to repeat themselves or speak louder.

Participating in Social Activities with Hearing Aids:

Social activities can be challenging for people with hearing loss, but hearing aids can make a significant difference. When participating in social activities, try to position yourself in a quiet area where you can hear conversations more clearly. Avoid loud environments, such as crowded restaurants or bars. If possible, inform your friends and family members about your hearing loss so they can make accommodations to help you.

Using Assistive Listening Devices with Hearing Aids:

Assistive listening devices, such as FM systems or captioned telephones, can be used in conjunction with hearing aids to improve your ability to hear. These devices work by transmitting sound directly to your hearing aids, reducing background noise and improving speech clarity.

Tips for Making the Most of Your Hearing Aid Experience:

There are several tips you can follow to make the most of your hearing aid experience, including:

Wear your hearing aids consistently: Wear your hearing aids as often as possible to get used to them and maximize their effectiveness.

Practice listening skills: Practice listening skills, such as focusing on one person's voice in a noisy environment, to improve your ability to hear in different situations.

Keep your hearing aids clean: Regularly clean and maintain your hearing aids to ensure they work effectively.

Seek support and resources: Join a support group or seek out other resources to connect with other hearing aid users and learn more about hearing loss and hearing aids.

Hearing aids can significantly improve your ability to hear and communicate, but it's important to use them effectively to get the most benefit. By communicating effectively with hearing aids, participating in social activities with hearing aids, using assistive listening devices with hearing aids, and following tips for making the most of your hearing aid experience, you can maximize the benefits of using hearing aids. Remember, hearing loss is a common problem, and there is no shame in seeking help. With the right support and resources, you can overcome the challenges of hearing loss and enjoy all of the sounds and experiences that life has to offer.

Chapter 7: Overcoming Stigma and Seeking Support

Hearing loss can be a challenging and isolating experience. Many people with hearing loss face stigma and social isolation, which can make it difficult to seek help and support. In this chapter, we will discuss how to overcome the stigma of hearing loss, finding support from family and friends, joining a hearing loss support group, and seeking professional counseling if needed.

Dealing with the Stigma of Hearing Loss:

Hearing loss is often stigmatized, and many people feel ashamed or embarrassed about their hearing loss. It's important to remember that hearing loss is a common problem, and there is no shame in seeking help. Don't let stigma prevent you from seeking the support and resources you need to improve your quality of life.

Finding Support from Family and Friends:

Family and friends can be an important source of support for people with hearing loss. Inform your loved ones about your hearing loss and how they can help. Ask them to speak clearly and face you when communicating, and avoid interrupting or talking over others.

Joining a Hearing Loss Support Group:

Joining a hearing loss support group can provide you with a sense of community and support from others who are experiencing similar challenges. Hearing loss support groups can also provide you with information about resources and services that can help you manage your hearing loss.

Seeking Professional Counseling if Needed:

Hearing loss can be a challenging experience that can cause emotional distress, such as anxiety or depression. If you're struggling to cope with your hearing loss, consider seeking professional counseling. A mental health professional can help you manage your emotional well-being and develop coping strategies to manage your hearing loss.

Hearing loss can be a challenging and isolating experience, but it's important to remember that there is help and support available. By overcoming the stigma of hearing loss, finding support from family and friends, joining a hearing loss support group, and seeking professional counseling if needed, you can manage your hearing loss and improve your quality of life. Remember, hearing loss is a common problem, and there is no shame in seeking help. With the right support and resources, you can overcome the challenges of hearing loss and enjoy all of the sounds and experiences that life has to offer.

Chapter 8: Hearing Aid Technology and Innovation

Advances in technology have led to significant improvements in hearing aid technology over the years. In this chapter, we will discuss advances in hearing aid technology, future trends in hearing aid technology, using hearing aids with other devices, and exploring the latest innovations in hearing aid technology.

Advances in Hearing Aid Technology:

Hearing aids have come a long way since their inception. Today's hearing aids are smaller, more powerful, and more advanced than ever before. Some of the advances in hearing aid technology include:

Digital processing: Digital processing allows hearing aids to filter out background noise and amplify speech, improving speech clarity.

Directional microphones: Directional microphones allow hearing aids to focus on sounds coming from a specific direction, improving speech understanding in noisy environments.

Bluetooth connectivity: Bluetooth connectivity allows hearing aid users to connect their hearing aids to other devices, such as smartphones or televisions.

Future Trends in Hearing Aid Technology:

The future of hearing aid technology is bright, with many exciting advancements on the horizon. Some of the future trends in hearing aid technology include:

Artificial intelligence: Artificial intelligence can be used to analyze sound and make adjustments to hearing aids in real-time, improving speech clarity and reducing background noise.

Biometric sensors: Biometric sensors can be used to monitor the wearer's physical activity, heart rate, and other health metrics.

In-ear language translation: In-ear language translation can translate foreign languages in real-time, allowing hearing aid users to communicate more effectively in international settings.

Using Hearing Aids with Other Devices:

Hearing aids can be used with a variety of other devices, such as smartphones, televisions, and music players. Bluetooth connectivity allows hearing aid users to connect their hearing aids to these devices, improving their ability to hear and communicate.

Exploring the Latest Innovations in Hearing Aid Technology:

There are many exciting innovations in hearing aid technology that are worth exploring. These include:

Rechargeable hearing aids: Rechargeable hearing aids eliminate the need for disposable batteries, making them more convenient and environmentally friendly.

Invisible hearing aids: Invisible hearing aids are nearly invisible when worn, making them a discreet option for people who are self-conscious about their hearing aids.

Self-adjusting hearing aids: Self-adjusting hearing aids can analyze sound in real-time and make adjustments to improve speech clarity and reduce background noise.

Advances in hearing aid technology have led to significant improvements in speech clarity and noise reduction, making them an essential tool for people with hearing loss. Future trends in hearing aid technology, such as artificial intelligence and in-ear language translation, hold promise for even further improvements. By using hearing aids with other devices and exploring the latest innovations in hearing aid technology, you can maximize the benefits of using hearing aids. Remember, hearing loss is a common problem, and there is no shame in seeking help. With the right support and resources, you can overcome the challenges of hearing loss and enjoy all of the sounds and experiences that life has to offer.

Chapter 9: Frequently Asked Questions about Hearing Aids

Hearing aids can be a confusing and overwhelming topic for many people. In this chapter, we will answer some common questions about hearing aids, dispel common myths and misconceptions, explain insurance coverage and hearing aid options, and provide resources for further information and support.

Common Questions about Hearing Aids:

What types of hearing aids are available?
There are several types of hearing aids, including behind-the-ear, in-the-ear, and completely-in-canal hearing aids.

Do I need a hearing test to get hearing aids?
Yes, a hearing test is necessary to determine the extent and type of your hearing loss, and to help determine the appropriate hearing aid for you.

How much do hearing aids cost?
Hearing aid costs can vary depending on the type and level of technology. Some insurance plans may cover the cost of hearing aids.

Myth-Busting Hearing Aid Misconceptions:

Myth: Hearing aids are big and bulky.
Reality: Hearing aids are now smaller and more discreet than ever before.

Myth: Hearing aids restore hearing to normal.
Reality: While hearing aids can significantly improve hearing, they do not restore hearing to normal.

Myth: Hearing aids are only for older people.

Reality: Hearing loss can occur at any age, and hearing aids can be beneficial for people of all ages.

Understanding Insurance and Hearing Aid Coverage:

Many insurance plans offer coverage for hearing aids, but the level of coverage can vary. It's important to understand your insurance coverage and the available options for hearing aids. Some options may include financing plans, discounts, and low-cost alternatives.

Resources for Further Information and Support:

There are many resources available for people with hearing loss and their families, including support groups, online forums, and educational resources. Your audiologist can also provide you with information and resources to help you manage your hearing loss and make informed decisions about hearing aids.

Hearing aids can significantly improve your ability to hear and communicate, but they can also be a confusing and overwhelming topic. By answering common questions about hearing aids, dispelling common myths and misconceptions, explaining insurance coverage and hearing aid options, and providing resources for further information and support, you can make informed decisions about managing your hearing loss and using hearing aids. Remember, hearing loss is a common problem, and there is no shame in seeking help. With the right support and resources, you can overcome the challenges of hearing loss and enjoy all of the sounds and experiences that life has to offer.

Chapter 10: Conclusion

Summary of Key Takeaways:

Throughout this book, we have discussed the importance of understanding hearing loss, the benefits of using hearing aids, getting started with hearing aids, adjusting to your new hearing aids, taking care of your hearing aids, maximizing your hearing aid experience, overcoming stigma and seeking support, exploring hearing aid technology and innovation, and answering frequently asked questions about hearing aids. Some key takeaways from this book include:

Hearing loss is a common problem that can significantly impact your quality of life.

Hearing aids can significantly improve your ability to hear and communicate.

It's important to work with an audiologist to determine the best hearing aid for you and to receive ongoing support and care.

Taking care of your hearing aids is essential for maximizing their lifespan and effectiveness.

There are many resources available for people with hearing loss and their families.

Encouragement to Seek Help for Hearing Loss:

If you are experiencing hearing loss, it's important to seek help. Don't let stigma or misconceptions prevent you from getting the support and resources you need to manage your hearing loss and improve your quality of life. Work with an audiologist to determine the best hearing aid for you and to receive ongoing care and support.

Final Thoughts and Recommendations for Using Hearing Aids:

Using hearing aids can significantly improve your ability to hear and communicate, but it's important to remember that hearing aids are just one tool for managing hearing loss. It's also important to communicate effectively, participate in social activities, and seek support when needed. By taking care of your hearing aids, maximizing your hearing aid experience, and seeking the right support and resources, you can overcome the challenges of hearing loss and enjoy all of the sounds and experiences that life has to offer.

Remember, hearing loss is a common problem, and there is no shame in seeking help. With the right support and resources, you can overcome the challenges of hearing loss and enjoy all of the sounds and experiences that life has to offer.

Bibliography:

American Speech-Language-Hearing Association. (2020). Hearing Loss and Hearing Aids. Retrieved from https://www.asha.org/public/hearing/Hearing-Loss-and-Hearing-Aids/

Better Hearing Institute. (2019). Frequently Asked Questions About Hearing Aids. Retrieved from https://www.betterhearing.org/hearingpedia/frequently-asked-questions-about-hearing-aids

Centers for Disease Control and Prevention. (2021). Hearing Loss. Retrieved from https://www.cdc.gov/ncbddd/hearingloss/index.html

National Institute on Deafness and Other Communication Disorders. (2021). Hearing Aids. Retrieved from https://www.nidcd.nih.gov/health/hearing-aids

Smaldino, J. J., & Forbis, S. G. (2017). Hearing Aids: A User's Guide. New York: Routledge.

Yueh, B., Shapiro, N., MacLean, C. H., & Shekelle, P. G. (2003). Screening and Management of Adult Hearing Loss in Primary Care: Scientific Review. JAMA, 289(15), 1976-1985. doi:10.1001/jama.289.15.1976